OnBoard
ACADEMICS

Consonants

© 2015 OnBoard Academics, Inc
Portsmouth, NH
800-596-3175
www.onboardacademics.com
ISBN: 978-1-63096-028-5

OnBoard Academic's books are specifically designed to be used as printed workbooks or as on-screen instruction. Each page offers focused exercises and students quickly master topics with enough proficiency to move on to the next level.

OnBoard Academic's lessons are used in over 25,000 classrooms to rave reviews. Our lessons are aligned to the most recent governmental standards and are updated from time to time as standards change. Correlation documents are located on our website. Our lessons are created, edited and evaluated by educators to ensure top quality and real life success.

Interactive lessons for digital whiteboards, mobile devices, and PCs are available at www.onboardacademics.com. These interactive lessons make great additions to our books.

You can always reach us at customerservice@onboardacademics.com.

Silent Consonants

Key Vocabulary

Silent consonants

Which letter is silent?

> Each of the consonant combinations **kn**, **gn**, **sc** and **wr** contain a silent letter that does not correspond to any sound in the word's pronunciation.

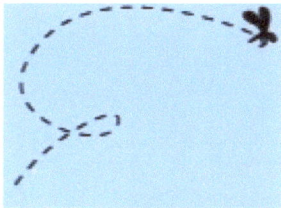

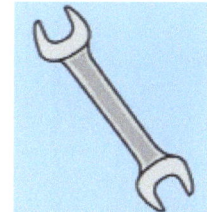

knife   **gnat**   **scissors**   **wrench**

☐   ☐   ☐   ☐

Silent consonant example

gn
Brian is a forei**g**n exchange student.

kn
The **k**night rode his black horse.

sc
There is a cre**sc**ent moon tonight.

wr
The dog **wr**estled with the toy.

Complete the word using a silent consonant pair.

☐ aw	☐ ent
☐ ob	☐ ee
☐ ite	☐ y

kn   **gn**   **sc**   **wr**

Write the silent consonant pair in the box next to the word.

☐ Sign

☐ Knack

☐ Ascent

☐ Wrong

☐ Align

☐ Wrath

Circle the Silent Consonants

Mia and I were hiking when she tripped on a gnarled root and scraped her knuckles. I knelt to wrap a bandage around her hand. The descent was hard, but we kept going because we knew it would be dark soon.

Fill in the blanks to identify the silent consonant.

☐ I used _____ to cut the rope.		knit
☐ We had _____ for dinner.		wreath
☐ The _____ smelled like pine.		lasagna
☐ The dog _____ on the bone.		gnawed
☐ Liz's mom _____ her a hat.		scissors

c   w   k   g

Name_____

Final Consonant Quiz

1. True or false? The word sister has a silent consonant.

2. Circle the word with the silent K: kangaroo   know
   kayak kabob

3. Circle the word that does NOT have a silent consonant:
   knot, wrote, strum, scene

4. Which word has a silent c: cane, back, scent, crash

5. What is the silent consonant in the word knife?

6. What is the silent consonant in the word knack?

7. Circle the word with the silent consonant: light, green,
   red, yellow

8. What is the silent consonant in the word wrong?

Consonant Blends

Key Vocabulary

consonant

consonant blends

Consonant Blends

Read the sentence and notice the spelling and sounds of the consonant blends in red.

A good friend makes you smile.

Please slow down.

Two consonant sounds that blend together are called *consonant blends*.

_____

Sort and Say
Write the consonant blends in the correct box. Say the sound after you write it in. Listen for both consonant sounds.

s_	_r	_l

(pl) (sp) (bl) (sl) (fl) (sm) (gr) (tr) (br)

Create the new words described by the picture by adding l or r to make consonant blends.

Write the word next to the picture.

side

fog

bush

tip

Fill in the missing consonant blends.

☐ apes   ☐ ain   ☐ ed

☐ oom   ☐ ell   ☐ ay

tr   sl   sp   br   pl   gr

Making words with consonant blends.
What words can you make with this consonant blend?

s	m			

s	m			

s	m			

s	m			

s	m			

Making words with consonant blends.
What words can you make with this consonant blend?

t	r			

t	r			

t	r			

t	r			

t	r			

Making words with consonant blends.
What words can you make with this consonant blend?

b	l			
b	l			
b	l			
b	l			
b	l			

Name_____

Consonant Blends Quiz

1. The word smart has a consonant blend. True or false?

2. Which blend can you use to complete the sentence?
   I went down the __ __ ide.
   a. sp
   b. gl
   c. sm
   d. sl

3. Which blend can you use to complete the sentence?
   We __ __ew the plane.
   a. sp
   b. br
   c. sm
   d. fl

4. Which blend can you use to complete the sentence?
   The dog had black __ __ ots.
   a. sp
   b. br
   c. sm
   d. fl

Final Consonant Blend

Key Vocabulary

Final consonant blend

Digraphs

How many sounds are in the final consonants.
Enter the number in the box and then identify the final consonants as a final consonant blend or digraph.

Final consonant blends: two consonant sounds at the end of a word.
Final digraphs: two consonants with a single sound.

nest ☐

fish ☐

hand ☐

munch ☐

Add a final consonant blend to complete each word.
Complete the word by adding the correct final consonant blend below.

pi___	la___	che___	ha___	cla___

_____

Organize the words by their final consonant blend. Say the word and listen to the sound of the final consonant blend.

sp	st	nd	nk	mp

TOAST	CAMP	GRASP	MEND	STAND	TANK	GASP
LIST	PLUMP	RINK	PUMP	LEND	BOAST	RANK

www.onboardacademics.com

Unscramble the final consonant blend words.

1	k n r i d
2	s f t i r
3	r i c s p
4	n l b e d
5	t a s p m

_____

Find rhyming words.

mend
s p e n d

last
p a s t

Name_____

Final Consonant Blend Quiz

1. True or False? Words with final consonant blends have two consonants with a single sound at the end.

2. What is the final consonant blend at the end of this word? CLAMP

3. What is the final consonant blend at the end of this word? BLAND

4. What is the final consonant blend at the end of this word? SKUNK

5. What is the final consonant blend at the end of this word? FIRST

6. What is the final consonant blend at the end of this word? STAMP

7. What is the final consonant blend at the end of this word? GRASP

8. Does the word "touch" end with a final consonant blend or a digraph?

Consonant Digraphs

Key Vocabulary

consonant

digraph

Digraphs

Read each sentence and listen to the sound and notice the spelling of the consonant digraph.

Look at **th**is **sh**ell, Mom.

It's **ph**enomenal! **Wh**ere did you find it?

At **th**e bea**ch**.

A digraph: when two consonants come together to make one sound.

Match and fill in the box each word containing a consonant digraph with the picture.
Circle the consonant digraph.

whale   thumb   shell   phone   chair

_____

Highlight or circle the digraphs.

Shelly collects shells.

Charlie chews chocolates.

Thor thinks he is thirsty.

Whitney watches whales.

Phil phones his friends.

Create words by connecting the boxes.
On which side are the digraphs?
Write the words below.

wh	ake
th	eck
sh	one
ch	ing
ph	ere

Complete the paragraph by filling in the blanks with words containing digraphs. Fill in the boxes with words containing these beginning digraphs.

Dad sat in a beach _____. It was too

hot, so he moved into the _____.

"_____ feels better," he said.

Mom took a _____ with her camera.

"I'll frame it _____ we get home,"

I said.

_____

th	ch	ph

wh	sh

Name_____

Consonant Digraphs Quiz

1. The word shape has a digraph. True or false?

2. Circle the digraph that you can use to complete the sentence. We had a __ __ at on the phone.
   a. ch
   b. th
   c. ph
   d. sh

3. Circle the digraph that you can use to complete the sentence. The child is __ __ ree years old.
   a. ch
   b. th
   c. ph
   d. sh

4. Circle the digraph that you can use to complete the sentence. __ __ o is coming over?
   a. Ch
   b. Th
   c. Wh
   d. Sh

Final Digraphs

Key Vocabulary

digraph

final digraph

Complete the word by adding the final digraph.

FI_____

BRO_____

IN_____

Match final digraph rhyming words.

1 beach				moth	latch
2 crash				cloth	cinch
3 sloth				wrath	lash
4 match				flinch	reach
5 bath				sash	batch
6 pinch				path	teach

Complete the word with the correct final digraph.

 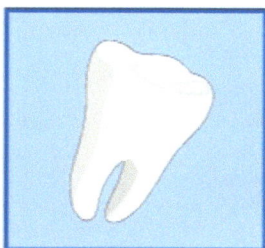 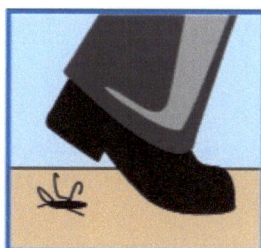 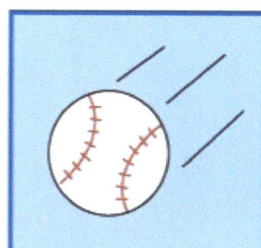

wat _____ ___   **too** _____ ___   **squi** _____ ___   **pit** _____ ___

th   **ch**   **sh**

Circle the objects whose name contains a final digraph.

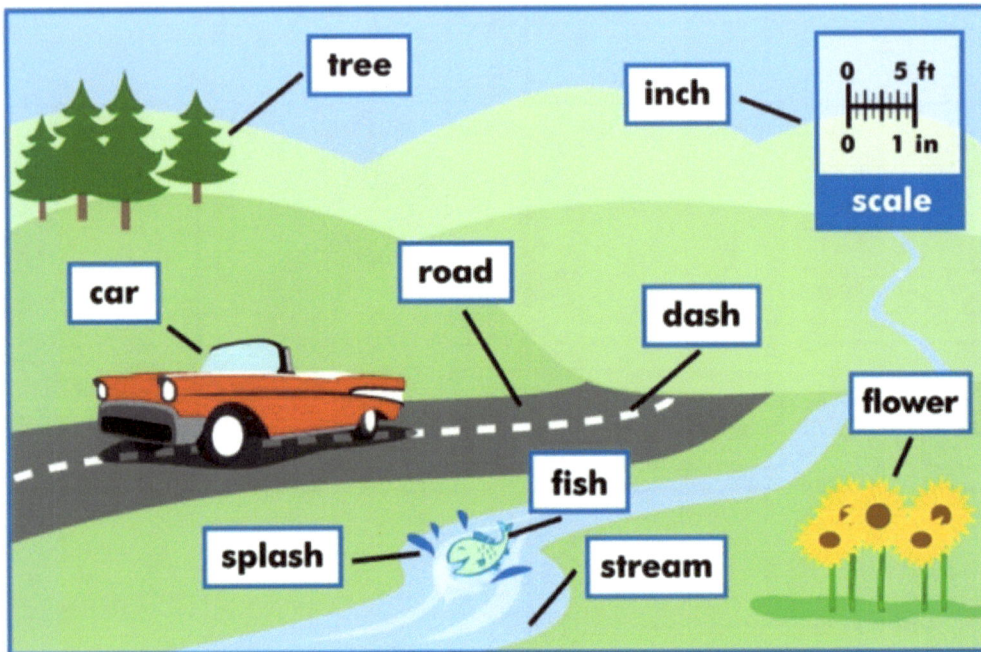

Can you guess my name?

I share my name with a famous baseball player whose nickname was Babe. My name ends with TH.

_____

My name rhymes with gosh and posh. My name ends with SH.

_____

My name is also a word that means having a lot of money. My name ends with CH.

_____

Final Digraph Crossword

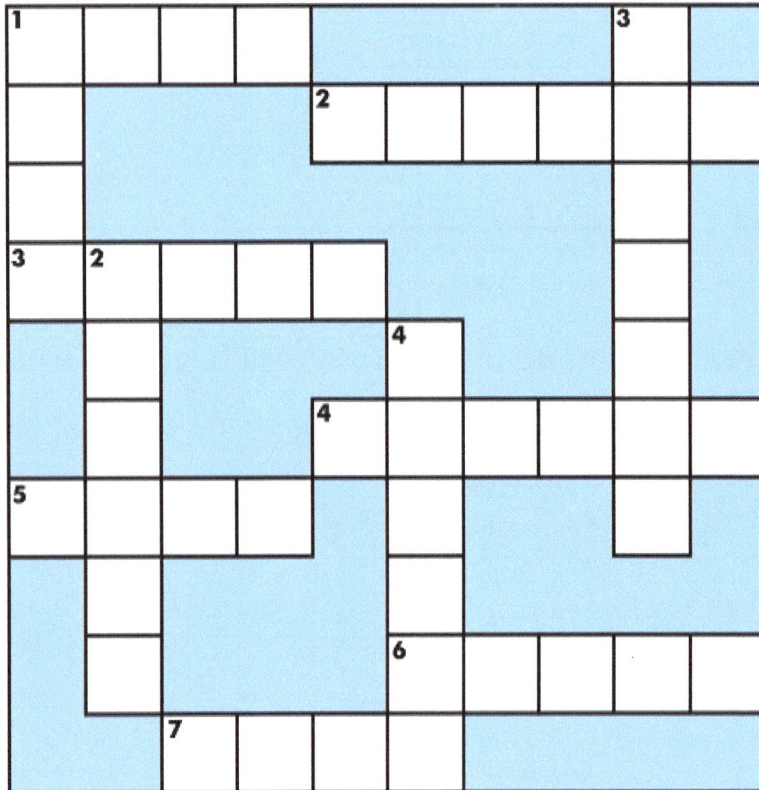

ACROSS

1. The 100 meter _____ .

2. You clean with this to disinfect.

3. When chicks break out of eggs.

4. How the _____ Stole Christmas.

5. Another word for money.

6. Taking out the _____ is a common chore.

7. You add and subtract during this subject.

DOWN

1. You eat dessert from this.

2. Staples will _____ pieces of paper together.

3. Car tires make this noise.

4. Period of rapid development, also called a _____ spurt.

Name_____

Final Digraph Quiz

1. True or false? The letters -ies form a final digraph.

2. Write the final digraph that you hear at the end of this word: WITH

3. Write the final digraph that you hear at the end of this word: BLOCK

4. Write the final digraph that you hear at the end of this word: BATH

5. Complete the word. Look at your wat_____ to check the time.

6. Complete the word. Deal the de_____ of cards.

7. Complete the word. Make a wi_____ upon a star.

8. Write the final digraph that you hear at the end of this word: CASH

Final Letter Patterns

Key Vocabulary

final letter pattern

Final Letter Patterns

These words have unique endings. The endings -tch, -ck, -dge, and -ng are called final letter patterns and always follow a vowel.

_____

Add the missing letters.

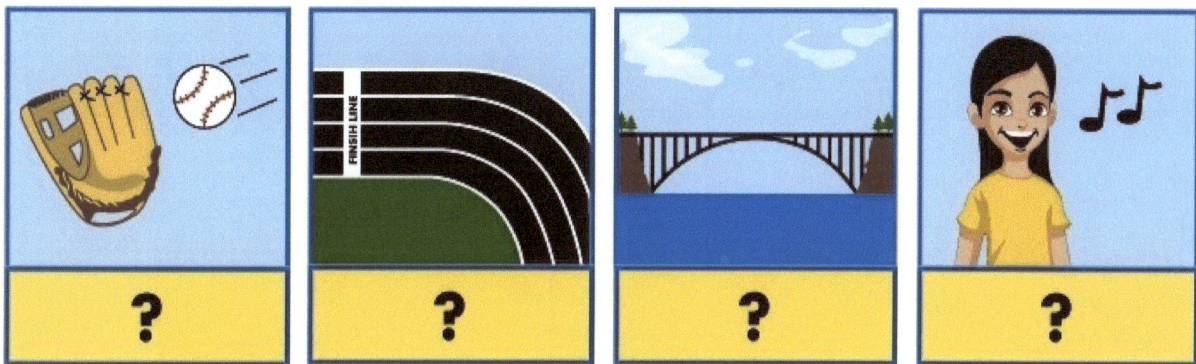

ca_____   tra_____   bri_____   si_____

| ng | tch | ck | dge |

Sort the words by their final letter pattern.

-tch	-ck	-dge	-ng

nudge	truck	song	sketch
ding	crutch	stuck	ridge

Create words using the final letter patterns shown in the boxes.

tch

ck

dge

ng

Circle the words with final letter patterns.

It was Saturday afternoon, and James was stretched on the couch watching the ⚾ baseball game. The phone rang. "James, it's for you," his mom called from the kitchen. James picked it up. "Have you raised any pledge money for the walk-a-thon?" Owen asked him. "Nearly," James answered. "I need one more pledge, but I am stuck." Owen replied, "You should have your mom make 🍪 a batch of chocolate chip cook-ies. That's how I got all my pledges!"

www.onboardacademics.com

Complete the Passage

Use an **-ng, -tch, -dge,** and **-ck** final letter pattern word
to complete this passage

We were in _____! We arrived just in time

to see the baby bird _____

from its egg. As we hid behind the

_____ , the first thing to emerge was one

tiny _____ .

Rhyming Words

Complete the table by adding rhyming words with the same final letter pattern.

patch		chick		fudge		king	

	tch		ck		dge		ng
	tch		ck		dge		ng
	tch		ck		dge		ng
	tch		ck		dge		ng

Name:_____

Final Letter Pattern Quiz

1. Select the correct spelling for a chocolate candy treat.
    a. fudj
    b. fudg
    c. fudge
    d. fudje

2. Select the correct spelling for an item used to attach paper to a bulletin board.
    a. tac
    b. take
    c. tack
    d. tak

3. She was a wi_____ for Halloween
    a. dge
    b. tch
    c. ng
    d. ck

4. Mom made a ba_____ of cookies
    4.1. dge
    4.2. tch
    4.3. ng
    4.4. ck